ART SMART

QED Publishing

Editor: Lauren Taylor
Design: Tall Tree Ltd www.talltreebooks.co.uk
Illustrator: Tom Connell

Copyright © QED Publishing 2012

First published in the UK in 2012 by
QED Publishing, a Quarto Group company
The Old Brewery
6 Blundell Street
London, N7 9BH

www.qed-publishing.co.uk

A catalogue record for this book is available from
the British Library.

ISBN 978 1 78171 089 0

Printed in China

At the top of the page for each project you will
find this handy key. It will tell you the difficulty
level to expect from each project:

Quick creative fix

These projects are quick, easy and perfect for
a beginner.

Sharpen your skills

Confident with your beginner skills? Move onto
these slightly tougher projects.

Ready for a challenge

For a challenging project you can really get
stuck into.

Creative masterpiece

Think you can tackle the toughest creative
projects? Have a go at these.

Note to adults:
Some children might be able to
do some or all of these projects
on their own, while others might
need more help. These are
projects that you can work on
together, not only to avoid any
problems or accidents, but also
to share in the fun of making art.

ART SMART

Traci Bunkers • **Kath Durkin** • **Melanie Grimshaw** • **Wendy Walker**

QED

QED Publishing

CONTENTS

FADING SHADING

Perfect your shading skills to create this layered pencil, moonlit landscape.

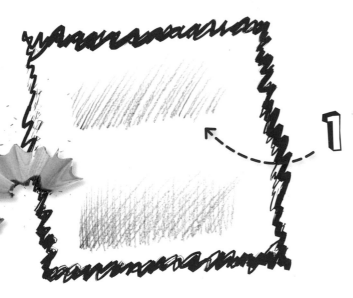

1 Practise shading with the side of a pencil point to make long strokes in the same direction. Try a soft pencil like a B or 2B, and don't press too hard. Add another layer over the first set, but going in a different direction.

2 Build up more layers of pencil in different directions and with strokes of different length until you feel confident shading from dark to light.

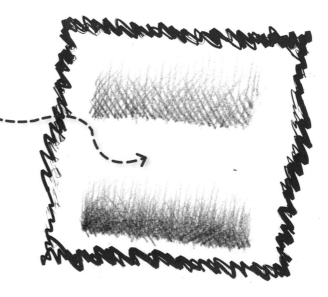

3 Draw out a 12 x 12 cm square. Draw some light, simple pencil lines from one side of the square to the other. Your lines might suggest sky, land, water, trees or buildings. Draw around a penny to make the moon.

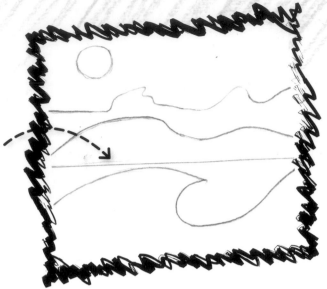

4 Begin your fading shading in the bottom shape. The fade can go upwards or downwards.

5 Make sure you shade each section in the same direction so that each one contrasts against the one next to it.

Sharpen your pencil regularly to keep your shading even.

FROTTAGE BUTTERFLIES

Build layers of textures and colours. Frottage comes from a French word, and means 'rub'.

1 Choose a textured surface and place a sheet of paper over it. With a coloured pencil or crayon, make a rubbing by colouring firmly over it with strokes in the same direction.

2 Experiment with all of your surfaces, using different colours and varying how firmly you make the rubbing.

3 Prepare a new sheet of paper with a background layer of one type of rubbing. Draw the outline of a butterfly with an HB pencil. You could trace a photograph of a butterfly, if you like.

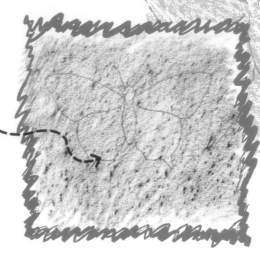

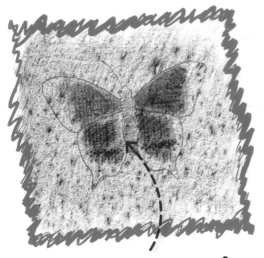

4 Add another layer of a different texture and in a different colour inside the wing shapes.

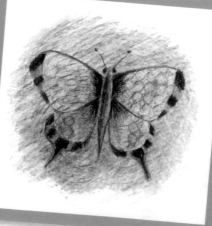

5 Have fun inventing the patterns and strong colours of your butterfly. Fill in all the shapes, using colouring pencils for the finer detail.

Netting, feathers, leaves, hessian, wood grain, wallpaper... you can make rubbings with so many things!

JUNGLE LINES

YOU WILL NEED:

- Paper
- Black fineliners in various thicknnesses
- HB pencil

Create a jungle full of exotic animals and plants. All you need is pencils and pens.

1 Practise drawing some lines with your pens. Experiment with creating textures and patterns. What type of lines make things appear closer or further away?

2 With a pencil, lightly draw the outlines of leaf and plant shapes. These are planning lines that you will not see on your final drawing.

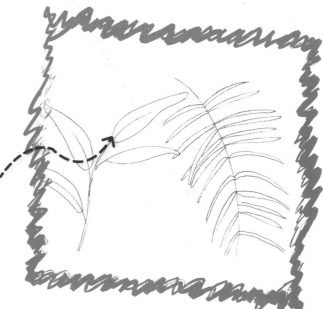

3 Add and overlap more jungle shapes at the bottom of the picture. This will form the foreground of your scene. Add tree trunks to the background too.

4 Look at the spaces you have left and imagine where you can place animals, hiding or peering out from behind the jungle plants. Keep adding more plants or flowers until it becomes a dense and exotic rain forest.

5 Redraw your planning lines using black fine liners. Look at your experiments from step 1 to help you decide which kinds of lines work best to describe the different areas of your jungle.

COOL CATS

Capture these cool, colourful characters for fun stickers.

YOU WILL NEED:

- Scissors
- Thick cartridge paper
- Gummed or sticker paper in various colours
- A black fineliner

1 Using the cartridge paper, draw and cut out a template of a cat's head to use over and over again.

2 Using sheets of different coloured gummed paper, draw around your template and cut out the cat's head shapes.

3 On a separate sheet of paper, practise drawing different faces and expressions.

4 Choose the faces you like best and draw them onto your cut-out heads.

5 You can stick your cool cats wherever you like! The repeat design would also make a brilliant wrapping paper.

Using a simple template is a quick way to make repeat patterns.

BLAST OFF!

Use simple perspective drawing to launch a rocket into space!

1 Begin by drawing a dot and a circle, some distance apart, using a pencil. You will need to erase them later.

2 Using a ruler, draw planning lines against the top and bottom curve of the circle to the dot. You will see a tube shape forming.

3 Draw another circle for a curved end to the tube shape, halfway down your planning lines.

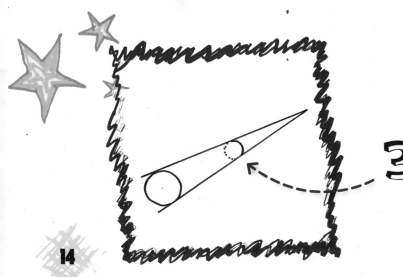
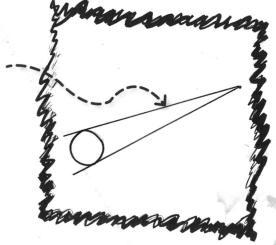

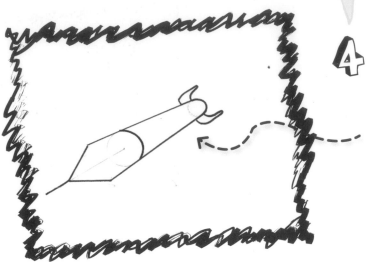

4 Turn the tube into a rocket by adding a triangular tip and some wings. Erase the planning lines and strengthen the lines you want to keep with darker pencil or pen. The dot becomes a planet millions of light-years away.

5 Use your imagination to add detail to build up your scene in colour

Sweeping lines and curves will add speed and movement to your drawing.

MAIL IT!

Send your postcard creations across the world or simply post them to yourself.

YOU WILL NEED:

- Postcard, used or new
- Collage materials, such as patterned paper, old stamps, pictures and stickers
- Scissors
- Glue
- Felt-tip pens
- Postage stamp

1 Decide on the sort of postcard you want. It could be old and written over, or blank so you can start from scratch.

POST CARD

2 Think about how you want to decorate your postcard. You could decide to say "Hello" in lots of different langauges.

hola

hi

hello

salut

konnichawa

hello

bonjour

ciao

3 You could use old envelopes with patterns, stamps, postmarks and torn edges to make a collage. Overlap your collage pieces to make a patchwork and think about how you want to fill in the spaces.

4 Arrange your collage before gluing it all into place on your postcard. You can use felt-tips or stickers to add more colour and interest.

Start a collection of scraps and any items that you find interesting to use for collage creations.

5 Make another collage for the other side of your postcard, and don't forget to leave space for the address. Now all you need to do is post it to the lucky recipient!

To: Alex Taylor
123 Any Street
Village Town
AAA 1BB

LEOPARD-SPOT PHOTO FRAME

Animal prints can make really great patterns and are easier to draw than you might think!

1 Draw a 12 x 12 cm square on your paper or card. Choose the colours for your fur base. Yellows, oranges, reddish browns and dark browns will work well. Working with the lightest colour first, begin to overlap your colours loosely, with long, fast strokes, to suggest a furry texture. Fill the whole square with your colours.

2 Practise drawing leopard spots. No two spots are exactly the same. They almost look like wiggly "O" and "C" letter shapes.

3 Carefully copy the spots onto your coloured square and fill them in with a dark colour.

4 Dip your finger into a saucer of water and use it to print furry "splodgy" effects on your spots. When it is completely dry, use the coloured pencils to add a final layer of scribbly, furry texture.

5 Cut out your coloured square and stick your photograph in the centre with a few drops of glue. Slide your picture carefully into the front of the CD case. It should fit perfectly and the frame will stand up on its own when it is left open.

What other types of animal print could you make?

MUSICAL DOODLES

Doodling to music stops you thinking too hard and allows your imagination to break free.

1 Put on your music and take a moment to clear your mind. When you feel ready, press your fingers onto the ink pad and make fingerprint rhythms that dance across the page. Do the rhythms you make change if you change the style of music?

2 Choose your favourite fingerprint rhythms and stare at the shapes. What do you see? Use felt-tip pens or fineliners to doodle the different characters you see. Maybe you see animals.

3 Add as much details as you like to your doodles, using a pencil first if you need more confidence.

4 Try varying the thickness of the lines you make to add more impact. Would dancing people be drawn with bolder lines than fluttering birds?

5 You could also try doodling on different types of paper. There's no limit to the different creations you can make when you free your imagination!

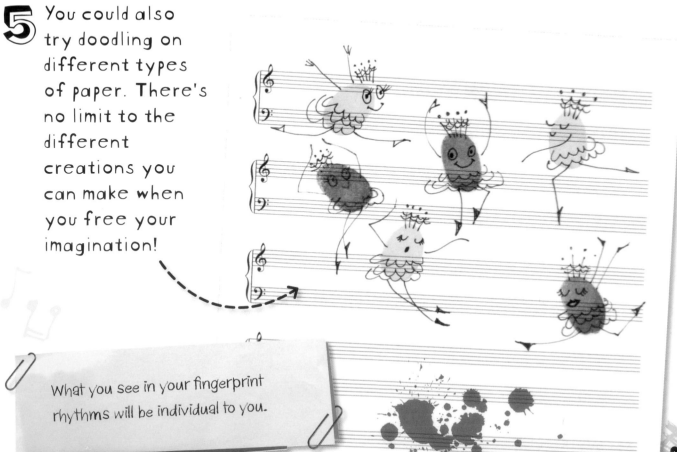

What you see in your fingerprint rhythms will be individual to you.

SPIRAL ART

What creative pictures can you make using only spirals?

1 Practise drawing spirals using a pencil. They can be quite loose or tightly curled.

2 Add a simple head and tail, and you have a snail with a spiral shell. Colour your snail with felt-tip pens, giving the spiral a shell pattern.

3 Use your imagination and find out what other pictures you can make using spirals. Always start with a simple spiral and see where you go from there.

4 Once you have found your favourite spiral drawings, you can build up a spirally scene. Here, spiral snails are crawling among spiral trees and plants. Colour your drawing to bring your scene to life.

Colouring spirals with patterns makes every one look different.

UP AND DOWN FACES

Facial expressions are always changing. Our faces can light **up** with joy or hang **down** with sadness.

1 Begin with an oval shape for a head. Find the middle of the oval and add two lines to make a cross. This shows where your features will be drawn.

2 To draw a happy face, mark lines for the eyes that go upwards at the corners on the eye line and a mouth that curves upwards. Add the eyebrows, eye shapes and lips.

3 Adding cheekbones and dimples will make the smile even stronger. Ears, nose and hair will complete the face.

4 Now make another face in the same way, but make the lines of the eyes and mouth go down at the corners.

5 Use a fineliner to strengthen your drawn lines and then erase the unwanted planning lines.

Making the angles more extreme will make an extremely happy or sad face!

SAY IT WITH FLOWERS

Create flowers with glitter glue and pastels for a special gift card.

YOU WILL NEED:

- Real flowers or pictures of flowers to study
- HB pencil
- 10 x 10 cm square of thick paper or card
- PVA glue or glitter glue in an easy squeezy bottle
- Coloured soft pastels
- Cotton buds
- An A4 piece of card
- Hair spray or artist's fixative

1 Before you begin your design, practise simple flower structures, by studying real flowers. Choose the flower shape you like best and draw its outline lightly with pencil to fit snugly onto your paper or card. Keep the shapes in your drawing really simple.

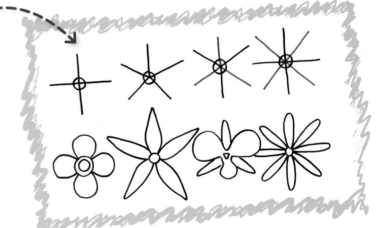

2 Draw over the pencil lines with the glitter glue. Touch the tip of the glue bottle directly onto the paper. Give a little squeeze and let the glue flow in an even line. Pulling the glue bottle towards you is always better than pushing it away from you. Let the glue dry completely.

3 Choose two different coloured pastels that will blend well together. One should be a deep colour and the other lighter. Working from the centre of the flower, add a little of the deep colour inside each of the petal shapes, then add the lighter colour to half fill each of the petals. Overlap the colours slightly.

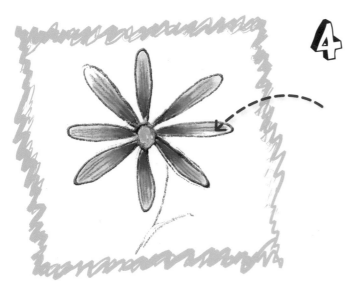

4 Carefully blend your colours with a clean finger or a cotton bud, ensuring that the colour stays inside the shapes and fades gradually out to the ends of the petals. You can add extra details with the edge of a pastel. Fix your drawing with hair spray or artist's fixative so that it doesn't smudge.

5 To make your drawing into a gift card, you will need to fold your piece of A4 card in half and carefully glue your drawing onto the front.

Draw a stem with multiple flowers on it, and colour them in the same way.

MICROSCOPIC ART

The world looks very different at a microscopic level. If you had microscopic eyes, what treasures would you find?

1 Begin with a single dot which will begin your 'microbe'. Make your microbe grow 'legs' with lines. Keep it simple to begin with by only using four legs. Then add more dots to the ends.

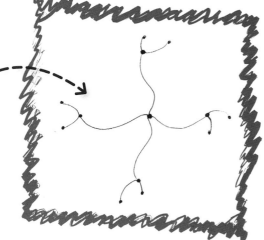

2 Make your microbe grow again from these new dots.

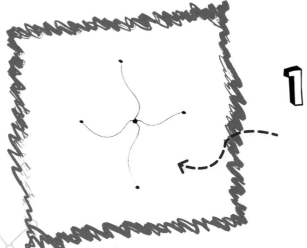

3 Keep adding and growing more legs from each dot. Make your microbe as big as you like.

4 Go back to the middle dot and begin to invent the body of your microbe.

5 Use your imagination to let it grow and grow, then add colour to bring life to your drawings.

Fill your paper with microscopic designs. What will your dots and lines become?

PICASSO SELF PORTRAIT

Picasso created weird and wonderful portraits. Here's how to make your own!

1 On tracing paper, draw a face-on portrait of yourself in pencil. Trace over a photograph of yourself or use a mirror.

2 On another piece of tracing paper, draw another portrait of yourself at the same size – this time from a profile view.

3 Draw a third portrait of yourself on another sheet of tracing paper at the same size – this time from a three-quarter turned view.

4 Take all three of your portraits and layer them on top of each other. Through the tracing paper, you should be able to see all three drawings. Line them up so your head is in the same place in each one.

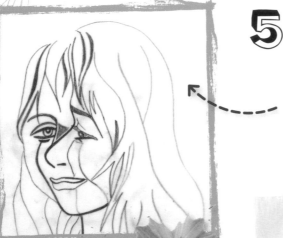

5 On a piece of cartridge paper, transfer your portraits (see page 110), picking out the different features to make a 'muddled' portrait. Thicken the lines you want to stand out.

Use acrylic paints to colour your portrait. The colours can be as strange as the portrait itself!

COLOUR WHEEL RUBBING

Explore the colours in a colour wheel with this rainbow design.

YOU WILL NEED:

- A variety of leaves
- Several thin sheets of paper
- Coloured pencils
- Watercolour paints
- Paintbrush

1 Collect some leaves from your garden or local park. Make sure they are different sizes and have some interesting patterns and textures.

2 Place your leaves under a sheet of thin paper, and practise making rubbings of them in different colours, using coloured pencils.

3 Next, arrange six similar-sized leaves in a fanned circle. Lay a clean sheet of paper on top and rub over the leaves in the colours of the colour wheel. These colours are: red, orange, yellow, green, blue and purple.

4 Using the watercolour paints and a paintbrush, practise blending out the six colours, so they go from bold to faint. Use more paint to make the colours bold and more water to make them fainter.

5 Finish your colour wheel by applying this painting technique around your leaf circle. Blend the different colours together when they meet to make new shades and tones.

Use this picture for colour reference when painting other projects.

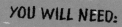

EASTER CHICK GIFTCARD

Combine painting and collage to make a bold design for a giftcard.

1 On a piece of cardboard, draw an Easter chick design using simple shapes. Make sure your design will fit on an A5 piece of paper.

Yellow acrylic, with gold metallic paint dabbed over the surface using a small strip of card

Orange and yellow acrylic mixed together to make a bold orange

A dark violet for adding strong details

2 On a separate piece of card, experiment with different colours of paint to decide how to colour your chick design.

Violet and white acrylic to make a pale purple

Eye

Head and beak

Wing

Body

Feet

3 Choose your favourite paint colours to paint the shapes of your chick. Once the paint is dry, cut these pieces out with scissors.

4 Assemble your pieces on your folded A4 cardboard. You can also add a background and a border decoration. Glue all the pieces into place.

You can make painted collage giftcards for any occassion! How about this scary pumpkin design?

DOODLE PAINTINGS

Doodling can free your imagination. You can get even more creative by painting the shapes you make.

1 Take your piece of paper and fineliner pen, and doodle a random line all around your paper. The line can circle, curl or zig-zag – anything you want!

2 When you've finished, look for pictures you could make from the shapes. If you look closely, this doodle could look like a duck and a mushroom.

3 Using your pen, fill in some extra details on the pictures you see in your doodle.

4 When you feel confident enough, paint your doodle picture to really bring it to life! You can experiment with your paints on a separate piece of paper first.

Every doodle you draw will make a new and exciting picture!

37

CREATE A MONSTER

Get imaginative with this monster character! Colouring with wax and paint can make great patterns.

1 To sketch out your monster character, draw egg shapes to make up the body, legs, arms and head.

2 Link them together and add details, such as fingers, toes, horns and facial features. You could even make him hairy!

3 Before you add colour to your monster, experiment on a separate piece of paper. Take a candle and draw patterns and textures that you'd like to use on your monster. Paint over the wax patterns with watercolour paint. The patterns you drew should come through.

4 Draw the wax patterns on your monster. Think about what patterns you want him to have on different parts of his body. Paint your monster with watercolour paints.

5 Finally, use a black fineliner pen to add definition and detail to your monster. You can even add a fantastic background!

Turn the page to the next project to give your monster a friend!

39

MONSTER PETS

In the last project you created your own monster. Now keep him company with a cool monster pet!

YOU WILL NEED:

- Cartridge paper
- HB pencil
- Acrylic paints, in various colours
- Textured materials to paint with, such as fabric, sponge and tinsel
- Paintbrush
- Paint palette
- Black fineliner

1 Begin by drawing egg shapes to make different characters. Use your imagination – they can look like whatever you want them to!

2 Work up these shapes, adding fur, scales, toes, eyes and antennae – anything you want!

3 Before you add colour to your monster pets, take a clean sheet of paper and experiment with different effects. Try painting with other things besides a paintbrush. These could be things like fabric, your fingers or sponges. Apply a small amount of paint to them and press or dab them onto the paper.

fabric textures

fingerprints

tinsel

sponge

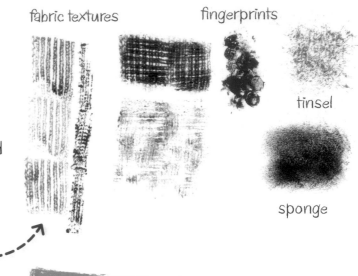

4 Choose your favourite painting techniques and use them to colour your monster pets. Think about what textures your different pets would have, depending on what features they have.

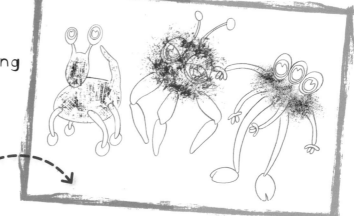

5 Finally, use a black fineliner pen to add definition and detail to your monster pets.

There's no limit to what your monster creations can look like!

GLOWING FISH

Using this unique painting technique, this colourful fish appears to almost glow.

1 First practise drawing fish shapes. Use rounded diamond shapes for the bodies and triangle shapes for the tails. Practise adding details, such as eyes, mouths, fins and scales.

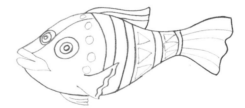

2 Draw your final big fish on your thick paper, then colour the fish and background using oil pastels and pressing very hard. Make it as colourful as possible and cover the entire paper. On a separate piece of paper, colour in a solid, smaller rectangle. This will be your test piece.

3 Take your black ready-made paint and paintbrush, and paint over your oil-pastel fish design. Cover the entire page, but leave a fine outline, so you can see where your fish drawing is. Paint over your test piece too. Let the paint dry completely.

 4 On your test piece, use your sharp object to scratch away at the paint to reveal the colours underneath. Experiment scratching out different patterns, using different tools to get different effects. Here are some suggested pattern ideas. Be very careful with anything you use that is sharp.

 5 Now scratch into your fish picture. If you feel confident enough, you can add more fish to make a full ocean scene.

Be careful not to scratch so hard that you go through the paper!

STENCIL SNOWFLAKES

Stencils are a fun and easy way to make loads of different patterns with paint.

1 Using the cups, draw two circles on a piece of thick paper. Cut the circles out, fold them in half, then fold them in half again.

2 On each of the folded circles, draw a different design. Cut out the shapes and unfold your circles.

3 Using sticky tack, stick your stencils to your cartridge paper. Lightly dip a cotton bud into the paint and dab all over the stencils. Peel the stencils off and wait for the paint to dry before adding more.

4 Ask an adult to help you with the spray paint. You must make sure you are in a large room with an open window or outside. Layer the stencils however you like. Stick your pencils to the paper, as before, and spray a light coat of paint over the top.

5 Layer your stencils any way you want. You can even stick them onto your painting afterwards for collage effect.

There are so many different shapes you can meake with circle stencils.

45

PERSONALIZED BOOKMARK

Use the initials of your name to make a funky design for a bookmark.

YOU WILL NEED:

- HB pencil
- Two sheets of thick card
- Ruler
- Scissors
- Watercolour paints
- Paint palette
- Small paintbrush

1 On your card, draw two horizontal lines 5 cm apart. Write your initials between these lines. Use a ruler to help you.

2 Using your ruler again, make the letters thick and chunky.

3 Using scissors, cut these letters out. You will use them as stencils for your bookmark.

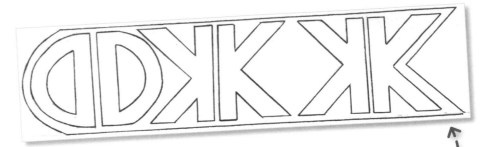

4 From your other sheet of card, cut out a strip 5.5 cm wide and 23 cm long. Use your stencils to create an interesting pattern on your bookmark. You can even flip them around and use them back to front.

5 Using watercolour paints, paint your bookmark using bright, complementary colours. Either yellow and purple, red and green, or blue and orange. Cut it out with scissors.

By arranging your initials in different ways, you can make bookmarks that have different shapes and patterns.

AMAZING MOSAIC

Create your own coloured and textured mosaics to make a cool mosaic design.

Paint mixed with sand

Thin paint applied with large brush

Dried paint with PVA glue patterns applied on top

Paint mixed with glitter

Paint swirled into patterns with fingertip

1 On the sheets of card, create different coloured or textured backgrounds. You can add sand or glitter to give the paint texture, or use your fingers or a sponge to make patterns. Let them dry completely.

Paint dabbed onto paper with small sponge

2 Using scissors, cut your coloured backgrounds into pieces. Try to cut them into shapes that will fit together easily, such as squares, rectangles and triangles. Make sure the largest pieces are no more than **4 x 4 cm**.

3 On a large sheet of cartridge paper, draw a 24 x 24 cm grid, and divide it up by **4 cm x 4 cm** squares.

4 Now get creative! Make a mosaic pattern by gluing the shapes onto the grid.

The patterns and colour combinations you can make are endless!

FRAMED SUNSET

YOU WILL NEED:

- Picture frame
- Pictures of sunsets for inspiration
- Large paintbrushes
- Acrylic paint, in various colours
- Paint palette

The artist Howard Hodgkin uses large brushes and sweeping brushstrokes to make paintings that look like sunsets.

1 Ask an adult to remove the glass from the picture frame, so you are left with the frame and backing only.

2 Look at your sunset pictures and decide on the background colours to paint your frame. Use large, horizontal brushstrokes to paint sweeping colour across the frame.

3 Once dry, choose other colours from your sunset pictures to layer over the background. Add these colours using the same sweeping brushstrokes.

4 Keep on layering colours until you are happy with your sunset. Remember to keep the brushstrokes loose and flowing.

5 Wait until your frame is completely dry before hanging on the wall!

Search on the Internet for 'Howard Hodgkin' to see beautiful sunset paintings just like yours!

PATCHWORK LANDSCAPE

Countryside landscapes can look a lot like patchwork. This inspired the artist David Hockney to make really colourful paintings.

YOU WILL NEED:

- Picture of countryside fields, for inspiration
- Masking tape
- Large piece of paper
- HB pencil
- Acrylic paints
- Paintbrush
- Paint palette
- Cotton buds

1 Look at your countryside picture and plan out your patchwork fields using light pencil lines. Stick lengths of masking tape around the edges of the paper. This will keep your painting neat.

Foreground

Middle

Background

2 Look carefully at the colours in your countryside picture. What shades would be best to use for the foreground, middle and background? Do the colours get paler as they move into the distance? Experiment with the colours you would like to use.

Grass: long, thin brush, dabbed onto paper on its side

Hedges: painting with a cotton bud

Cornfields: bold red and yellow stripes

3 On a separate sheet of paper, experiment with the brushstrokes you can make to suggest different parts of the landscape.

4 Paint your landscape, one patchwork square at a time. Use your experiments to decide what colours and techniques to apply to each area.

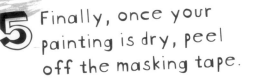

5 Finally, once your painting is dry, peel off the masking tape.

You could even paint the scene outside your window.

PRINTED PET T-SHIRT

You can liven up plain T-shirts with this easy printing method.

YOU WILL NEED:

- Cardboard or folded newspapers
- T-shirt, washed
- Fabric paints, in various colours
- Flat paint palette
- Sponge brush
- Small paintbrush

1 Insert a piece of cardboard or folded newspapers inside the T-shirt. This will stop the paint soaking through to the back. Make sure the shirt is smooth and not wrinkled.

2 Squeeze some paint onto your paint palette, then use a sponge brush to spread it into a thin layer. Use several colours for a more vibrant design.

3 Draw a picture of your pet, or a favourite animal, into the paint with a paintbrush. Everything will print backwards, so if you include any writing, be sure to write it backwards.

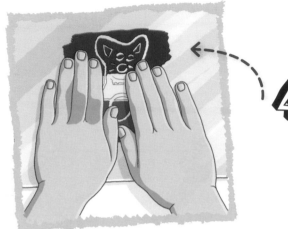

4 Carefully place the painted side of the paint palette on the T-shirt where you want the design to print. Press down on the palette to be sure the whole picture will print.

5 Carefully peel the palette off the T-shirt and let the paint dry. Heat-set the design according to the directions on the fabric paints.

Practise your design on paper first to get the best outcome!

PICTURE PERFECT

Decorate a picture frame with stamps you can make and change yourself!

 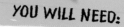

- Poster paints, in various colours
- Plastic cup
- Unvarnished wooden picture frame, with backing and glass removed
- Paintbrush or sponge brush
- Modelling clay
- Sharp pencil and items to make texture
- Thin sponge

1 Pour a small amount of light coloured paint into the plastic cup. Paint the front and sides of the frame with the paint. Let it dry.

2 Roll a small piece of modelling clay into a short log shape. Pinch one end to make a small handle and flatten the other end for the stamp.

56

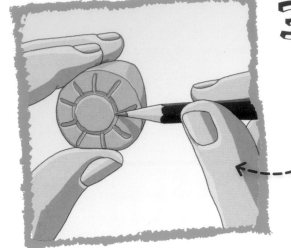

3 Use a pencil to draw a design into the flat part of the stamp. You could also make a texture by pressing different items into the clay, such as a straw or the pattern on the sole of a shoe.

4 Squeeze a small amount of paint onto the sponge. Use your fingers to spread it around. Press the stamp onto the paint on the sponge, then stamp onto the frame. Repeat to create whatever pattern you like.

5 When the frame is dry, you can stamp the frame again using a different colour or design.

This would make a unique gift!

COOL KID SHOES

Impress everyone with these arty shoes that you painted yourself.

1 Stuff the shoes with scrunched-up newspaper so that they hold their shape. Apply the masking tape to make a stripy pattern on the shoes.

2 Squeeze a small amount of paint onto a paper plate. Dip the paintbrush into the paint, then tap the brush between the masking tape stripes to colour in the spaces.

3 When the paint is dry, remove the masking tape.

4 Place the stickers onto the unpainted areas of the shoes. Using a different paint colour, tap the paint brush around the edges of the stickers, colouring in the stripes.

5 When the paint is dry, remove the stickers. Add some decoration with fabric pens or colour in the white shapes, if you like.

Add some funky laces to make your shoes even more colourful.

ARTIST'S SELF-PORTRAIT

Every artist should make a self-portrait, and printing gives you a unique way to do it!

YOU WILL NEED:

- Large piece of cardboard
- Scissors
- Sheet of paper
- PVA glue, in a squeezy bottle
- Thick wool or string
- Acrylic paint
- Plastic cup
- Sponge brush
- Crayons, felt-tip pens and glitter glue

1 Cut your cardboard a little smaller than your piece of paper. Draw your self-portrait onto the cardboard using a felt-tip pen.

2 Trace over the lines of your self-portrait drawing with PVA glue, then press the thick wool or string into the glue. Let the glue dry.

3 Pour a small amount of paint into the plastic cup. Dip your sponge brush into the paint, then brush it onto the glued wool.

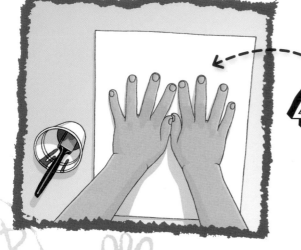

4 Before the paint dries, place your paper on top of the self-portrait. With your hands, push down on the paper, carefully moving your hands around so that the paint prints onto the paper.

5 Lift the paper off the printing cardboard and let the paint dry. Decorate your printed portrait with things like crayons, felt-tip pens and glitter glue.

You can use this method to create a picture of anything you like!

WICKED WRAPPING PAPER

Printing is great for creating repeating patterns - perfect for making your own wrapping paper!

YOU WILL NEED:

- Felt-tip pen
- Adhesive craft foam
- Scissors
- Empty cylindrical tin, with label left on
- Masking tape
- Poster paints, in various colours
- Paint palette
- Sponge brush
- A large sheet of paper

1 Draw some simple shapes, such as stars, hearts and zigzags, on the craft foam. Cut the shapes out with scissors.

2 Ask an adult to tape the lid back on to the tin with masking tape. This will help it hold its shape.

3 Stick the foam shapes onto the tin, leaving about 2 cm free at each end for rolling with your hands.

4 Squeeze some paint onto your paint palette. Apply the paint onto the foam shapes with the sponge brush.

5 Roll the tin over the paper, printing the foam shapes pattern. Apply more paint when you need to. When the paint is dry, use a different colour to print on top of the first layer.

You can make so many different designs with this method!

TERRIFIC TREASURE BOX

Transform a simple box into a colourful treasure box to store all your odds and ends.

YOU WILL NEED:

- Cardboard box with lid
- Poster paints, in various colours
- Small dish of water
- Paint palette
- Paintbrush
- Pencil
- Pop-up sponges (alternatively, use any thin sponge)
- Scissors
- Crayons, felt-tip pens and glitter glue (optional)

1 Paint the box and lid one colour.

2 Draw some simple shapes onto the pop-up sponges with a pencil, then cut them out with scissors.

3 Place the sponge shapes in water to let them expand. Then squeeze the water out of them. You won't need to do this if you're using normal sponge or foam.

4 Pour a small amount of paint onto your palette. Dip the sponge stamps into the paint so that the bottom surface is covered, then stamp it onto the box or lid. Stamp your box with different colours and stamps to make the pattern you want.

5 When the paint is dry, you can decorate your box with crayons, felt-tip pens, glitter glue or anything else you'd like.

You can decorate the inside of the treasure box too!

BRILLIANT BIRTHDAY CARDS

When you make your own birthday cards, you can personalize them for the lucky recipient.

YOU WILL NEED:

- Construction paper for card and for stencil
- Scissors
- Sticky tape
- Acrylic paint
- Plastic cup
- Fat paintbrush
- Crayons, stickers, felt-tip pens and glitter glue

1 For the stencil, draw a small, simple outline of a picture on the paper that you can cut out.

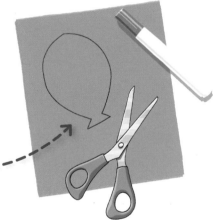

2 Cut a straight line to the picture from the edge of the card, then carefully cut the shape out, ending back at the straight line. Tape the paper back together along the cut line, completely covering the cut.

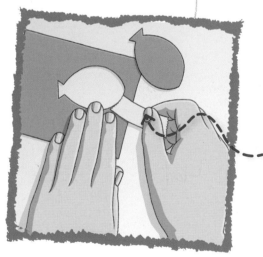

3 Fold the paper for the card in half, then open out flat. Place the stencil on the right half of the card.

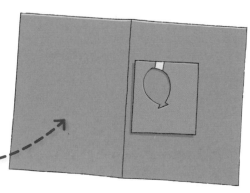

66

4 Pour a small amount of paint into the plastic cup. Dip the paintbrush into the paint. While holding the stencil down with one hand, tap the brush around the inside and edges of the cut-out area. Do this until the whole shape is filled in with paint.

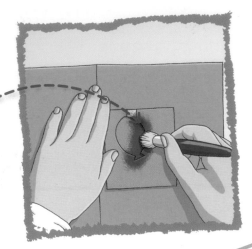

5 Lift the paper stencil off and let the paint dry. Repeat with different colours until you are happy with the design. When the paint is dry, personalize the card with crayons, stickers, felt-tip pens and glitter glue.

happy birthday

happy birthday

The shape cut out of the stencil can be used as a mask. Use it like a stencil, tapping the paint around the edges of the shape.

PRINTED GIFT STICKERS

Customize your own gift stickers using floral foam.

1 Draw a simple design onto one side of the floral foam, piercing the surface of the foam with the pencil as you draw. Carve out a rectangular space at the bottom, leaving a border. This will leave a space to write in.

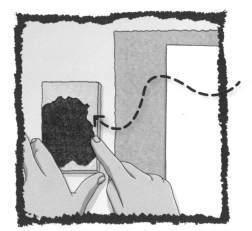

2 Squeeze a small amount of paint onto a sponge, then use your fingers to spread it around the surface. Place a piece of testing paper on top of a folded towel.

3 Press the carved side of the floral foam onto the paint on the sponge, then stamp it onto the test paper. If the design is faint in areas, redraw it into the foam, piercing deeper. Test the stamp again. You might need to do this a few times to get a print you are happy with.

4 Place the label paper on top of the towel. Press the foam onto the paint sponge and stamp onto the label paper. Repeat this until the label paper is covered. Add more paint to the sponge when needed.

5 Use felt-tip pens to colour in the white areas of the stamps. Finally, cut the sheet into individual gift stickers.

Jack   Olivia   Ruby   Thomas

Perfect for Christmas if you need to tag a lot of presents!

VEGGIE-PRINT BAG

Design your own bag using printing objects from around your home.

YOU WILL NEED:

- Fabric bag
- Cardboard or folded newspapers
- Fruits or vegetables, such as an orange and carrot
- Acrylic paints, in various colours
- Plastic cups
- Sponge brush
- Knife (and an adult to help you!)
- A toy car or other objects from around the home with interesting shapes, textures or patterns

1 Lay the bag flat and put a piece of cardboard or folded newspapers inside it. This will stop the paint from soaking through to the other side. Make sure the bag is smooth and not wrinkled.

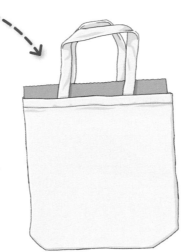

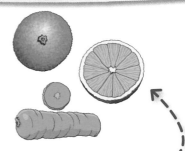

2 Ask an adult to cut some fruits or vegetables in half or into small pieces. Remove any seeds.

3 Squeeze a small amount of paint into a plastic cup. Dip the sponge brush into the paint, then brush it onto the cut side of a piece of fruit or vegetable.

4 Press the fruit or vegetable stamp onto the bag. Continue printing with different pieces and colours, making a picture or design. Let it dry, then print the other side of the bag.

5 With a foam brush, brush paint onto the wheels of a toy car. Roll the wheels along the fabric to make printed tyre tracks. You can use almost any object or toy you like to print with, but remember to ask for permission first!

Don't eat any of the fruits or vegetables that you have painted!

PERSONALIZED STATIONERY

Print your own stationery for letters, thank you notes or invitations!

YOU WILL NEED:

- Blank stationery paper and envelopes
- Small toys or household objects for stencilling
- Acrylic paints, in various colours
- Plastic cups
- Fat paintbrush
- Sponge brush

1 Open the stationery paper and place it flat, with the outside facing up, in the direction you want the card to be. Place the object to be used as a stencil on the half of the card that is the front. Here, a flat plastic animal figurine has been used.

2 Squeeze a small amount of paint into a plastic cup. Dip the paintbrush into the paint. While holding the object on the paper with one hand, tap the brush around the edges of the object and any cut-out areas. Do this until the whole shape is stencilled with paint.

3 After the paint is dry, stencil again on a different area with the same object, or a different one. Use a different colour of paint if you like. You can also stencil the half of the card that is the back.

4 You can also try printing the objects instead of stencilling. With a sponge brush, apply paint onto the object. Stamp the object onto the paper, pressing down all of the edges. Repeat as many times as you like.

5 Stencil and stamp the envelope to match.

Be creative - there are loads of colours and designs to choose from.

BUBBLE WAND BOARD

Liven up a plain bulletin board with colourful stencilling.

YOU WILL NEED:

- Acrylic paints, in various colours
- Plastic cups
- Paintbrush or sponge brush
- Cork bulletin board
- Large bubble wands with shapes
- Fat paintbrush
- Paper towel
- Old toothbrush
- Felt-tip pens

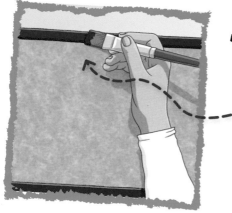

1 Squeeze a small amount of paint into a plastic cup. Add a little water to thin the paint and stir. Paint the front and frame of the bulletin board. Let it dry.

2 Squeeze a small amount of a different coloured paint into a cup. Place a bubble wand where you want it on the bulletin board. Dip the fat paintbrush into the paint. Hold the bubble wand flat with one hand and tap the brush in all the cut-out spaces of the bubble wand.

3 Clean the bubble wand with a damp paper towel. Repeat the previous step, using a different colour paint if you like, this time with the wand in another place. Continue stencilling with the same wand, or another one, until you have a design you're happy with. Remember to let the paint dry before stencilling on top of another design.

4 After the paint is dry, you can add to the design with felt-tip pens.

5 To finish, create a splatter pattern. Squeeze a small amount of paint onto an old toothbrush. With the bristles facing down, run your finger across the bristles towards you to splatter paint on the bulletin board.

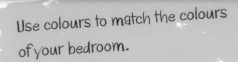

Use colours to match the colours of your bedroom.

SUPER SKETCHBOOK

Every artist needs a sketchbook. Here's how to make your own!

YOU WILL NEED:

- Scissors
- Cardboard
- Heavy paper for the cover
- PVA glue in a squeezy bottle
- Crayons
- Paper for inside the book, about 5-8 sheets
- Hole punch
- Ribbon or wool, three times the length of the book
- Felt-tip pens and glitter glue

1 Cut the cardboard a little smaller than the paper for the cover. Draw any design you like onto the cardboard.

2 Trace over the lines of your picture with PVA glue and let it dry. The glue should dry in raised, hard lines. This is your rubbing plate.

76

3 Put the cover paper on top of the rubbing plate. Rub over it with crayons to make the design appear, filling the whole paper.

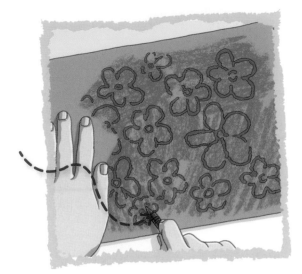

4 Stack the cover and the inside paper together, and fold them in half. Open them back up. Punch a hole about 2 cm from each end on the fold. You will need to punch several sheets at a time instead of all of them together.

5 Stack the cover and pages together again. String the ribbon or wool through the holes. Tie snugly on the outside to hold the book together. Decorate your sketchbook with felt-tip pens and glitter glue.

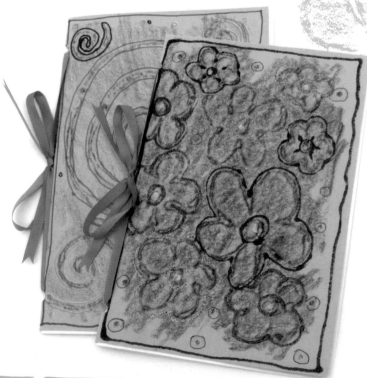

Using lined paper instead of blank for the inside pages, you can also make a journal.

LOVE-HEART GIFT BOX

Is a special occasion coming up? This cute gift box will be a great way to present your gift!

1 For the heart, cut out two equal-sized pieces of felt. Pin these two pieces together.

2 Using a needle and thread, stitch the heart pieces together using blanket stitch. Leave a small space to insert your toy stuffing, then stitch it completely closed when you have stuffed the heart.

3 Wrap a length of ribbon around the outside of your box, and secure it with fabric glue. You could also stitch on one or two separate felt heart shapes to the ribbon.

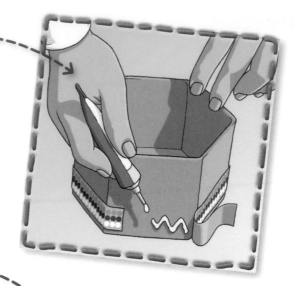

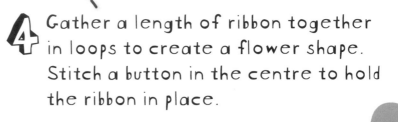

4 Gather a length of ribbon together in loops to create a flower shape. Stitch a button in the centre to hold the ribbon in place.

5 Finally, glue the stuffed felt heart and ribbon flower to the box lid using fabric glue.

Make an Easter-themed box using colourful feathers for a cute Easter chick!

WOVEN MOBILE

This mobile will add a splash of colour to your bedroom, and it's great fun to make!

YOU WILL NEED:

- Balls of wool in assorted colours
- Wooden dowel rods of various lengths
- Scissors
- Coloured beads

1 With the end of a small ball of wool, tie a knot around the centre of two dowel rods. Secure the rods into a cross shape.

2 Weave the wool over and around one dowel rod, then over and around the next, and so on with each rod. Make sure to keep the wool taut and keep your rods in the cross position.

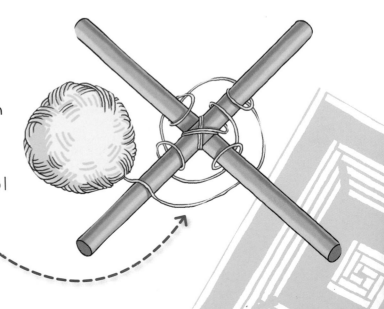

3 Keep weaving and tie on new colours of wool to make a stripy effect. Stop when you have a few centimetres of space left at both ends of each rod. Tie the loose end of the wool in a knot to secure it.

4 Make a variety of different-sized woven crosses and tie them together with wool to make a hanging mobile. Finally, thread colourful beads onto any loose ends of wool for decoration.

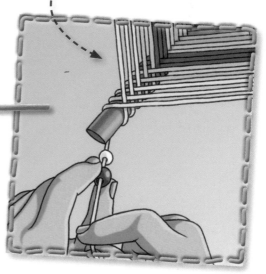

You can use different colours to match the colours of your bedroom!

SPACE PILLOWCASE

Want to create a theme for your bedroom? Printing on fabric can liven up plain pillowcases.

1 Cut a piece of cardboard to fit inside your pillowcase. Insert the cardboard into the pillowcase and lie it flat.

2 Squeeze different fabric paint colours onto separate paper plates.

82

3 Use objects, such as sponges, cotton spools and cardboard shapes, to print with. Dip them into the paint and press them onto the fabric. You can cut out rocket ship or star shapes from sponge and cardboard.

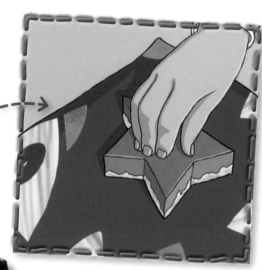

4 Print your pattern all over the front of the pillowcase. Once dry, turn over and repeat on the back.

5 Once completely dry, ask an adult to place a thin cloth over the pillowcase and slowly iron over it on a cool setting. This will seal the paint and stop it from cracking or washing off.

Get creative and use any colours and printing objects you like. How about a nature pattern?

POCKET ORGANIZER

Keep your bedroom tidy and stylish at the same time with this fun organizer.

YOU WILL NEED:

- Scissors
- An old piece of clothing that has pockets
- Felt in assorted colours
- Pins
- Needle
- Embroidery thread
- Fabric glue
- Sequins and goggly eyes
- Long length of ribbon
- Wooden dowel rod

1 Cut a large rectangle from an old piece of clothing, including the pockets.

2 Cut out decorative felt shapes and pin these in place on the fabric. Stick on goggly eyes if you have made any animal shapes.

leaves

animal shapes

eyes

84

3 Stitch on the shapes using running stitch. You can also glue or stitch on sequins to decorate your shapes.

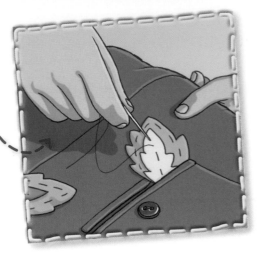

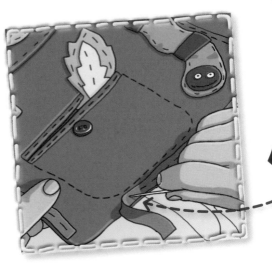

4 Using running stitch, sew a length of ribbon around the edge of the organizer to hide the rough edges and create a border.

5 Stitch two loops of ribbon to the top of the organizer and slip a wooden dowel rod through the loops so it can be hung.

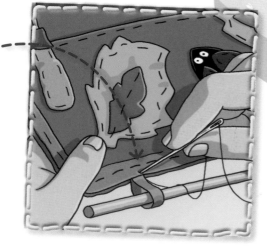

Create felt shapes that show your favourite theme. The more colourful, the better!

HAIR BAND BIRD

You can create this cute, colourful bird for a show-stopping hair accessory.

1 Cut out two equal-sized pieces of felt for the main body shape of your bird. Pin these two pieces together.

body pieces

2 Using a needle and thread, stitch around the outside of the body in either blanket or running stitch, leaving a space of about 1 centimetre open.

3 Through this space, fill the body with toy stuffing, then stitch up the hole.

4 Cut out felt ovals for the face, a folded diamond for the beak and triangles for the feathers and ears. Glue or stitch these onto the body.

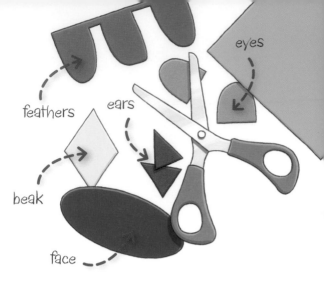

feathers

ears

eyes

beak

face

5 Attach feathers for wings and a pair of goggly eyes to make your bird come to life! Finally, stitch a hair band to the back of the bird's body.

Make a pencil tidy, using different felt shapes and colours to create any animal you want!

GET WELL CARD

This cute, colourful card will really brighten someone's day.

1 Lay three of the felt squares side by side and sew them together in turn, using running stitch. Do this by holding two squares together and stitching along the very edge of one side. Repeat with the third square.

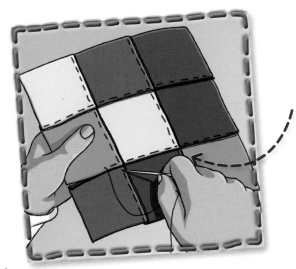

2 Repeat with the other squares to make three rows. Sew the rows together in the same way. Flip the quilt over so the stitching is on the back. Add running stitch around the edge for decoration.

3 Make a small pillowcase by cutting out a rectangle of white felt and decorating around the edge in running stitch.

ears and nose

face

cheeks

quilt edge

hands

4 Cut out felt shapes for the face and hands. Stitch eyes and a mouth onto the face circle and glue this onto the pillowcase. Cut a strip of white felt to make a quilt edge to position the hands onto.

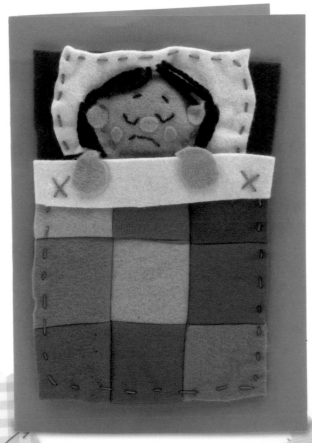

5 Using an embroidery needle, sew wool around the head to make hair. Glue all the felt pieces onto a rectangle of backing felt and glue onto a folded piece of A4 card.

Who wouldn't feel better after receiving a beautiful card like this?

DINO DOORSTOP

This colourful fabric dinosaur will make the perfect little guard for your bedroom door.

1 With tailors' chalk, draw four equal-sided triangles on the patterned fabrics and felt. Make sure each side of each triangle is 15 cm long. Cut out the triangles.

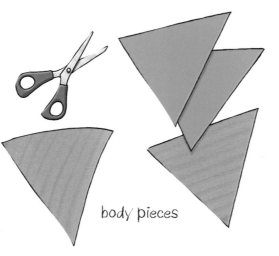

body pieces

2 With the patterned sides facing inward, use running stitch to sew the triangles together at the sides to make a pyramid shape. Leave the final side open and turn the pyramid the right way around.

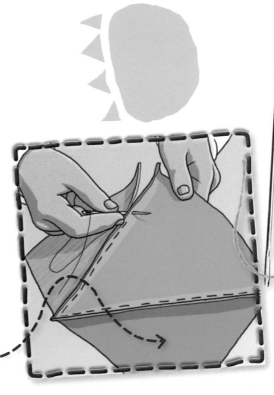

3 Through the open side, fill the pyramid with dried beans. (You can use a paper cone to do this.) Sew up the open side with blanket stitch.

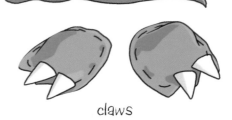

tail

claws

4 Make a stuffed felt snout, two hands and a tail using felt shapes sewn together with running stitch and stuffed with toy stuffing. Stitch these pieces onto the pyramid body.

5 Cut out features, such as spikes, teeth, claws, eyebrows and spots, from felt and a sheet of foam. Glue these onto the body, then stick on a pair of goggly eyes to bring your dinosaur to life!

Make a cuddly dinosaur instead by replacing the dried beans with toy stuffing.

TWISTY SOCK SNAKE

This twisty snake is cute, colourful and super-easy to make.

YOU WILL NEED:

- A sock
- Toy stuffing
- A pipe cleaner
- Elastic bands, about 6
- Needle
- Embroidery thread
- Scissors
- Felt, in assorted colours
- Fabric glue
- Colourful beads
- Goggly eyes

1 Fill a sock with toy stuffing and insert a pipe cleaner through the middle, so it is contained inside.

2 Tie about six elastic bands at 5 centimetre intervals along the sock to create the round sections of the snake's body.

3 Sew a line of loose running stitch around the opening and pull the end of the thread until it gathers closed. Secure by tying a knot in the thread.

92

4 Cut out felt shapes to add to your snake, such as a pink forked tongue and diamond shapes to decorate its back. Sew or glue these into position.

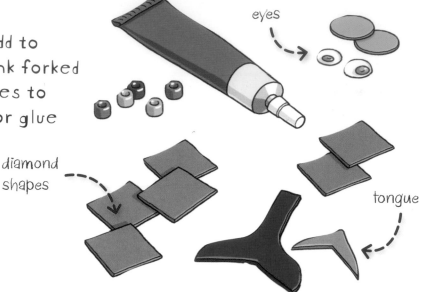

eyes

diamond shapes

tongue

5 Finally, add some finishing touches to your snake. Sew on colourful beads for decoration and add goggly eyes to bring him to life.

A patterned sock will make your snake even more interesting.

PATCHWORK PICTURE

Pictures don't have to be painted. You can create a 3D picture using fabrics instead.

YOU WILL NEED:

- An A5 wooden picture frame, glass and backing removed
- String
- Staple gun and staples
- Scissors
- Paper
- Pins
- Assorted green, patterned fabrics
- Green and black felt
- Needle
- Embroidery thread
- Toy stuffing
- Long length of blue and purple wool and ribbon
- Fabric glue
- 2 x White and grey pom poms (see page 28)

1 Wrap string around your frame, leaving **1-centimetre** spaces between the lengths. Staple the threads to the back of the frame and cut off the lengths at the front.

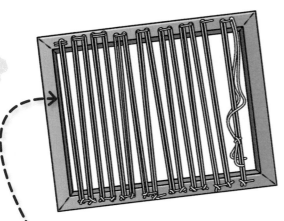

2 Cut out about five hill shapes from paper and use these as templates to cut out hills from patterned fabrics and felt. Make sure the hills will fit in the lower half of your frame.

94

3 Sew the fabric hills onto a 20 x 8-centimetre rectangle of green felt, using running stitch. Leave a space in each to insert a small amount of toy stuffing before sewing them closed. Trim the top of the backing felt into a curved hill shape.

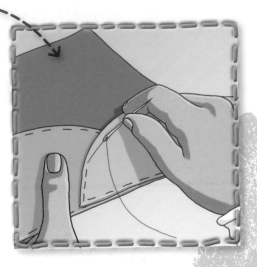

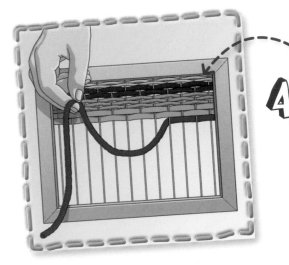

4 To make the sky, weave the ribbon and wool through the lengths of string on the frame until half the frame is filled.

head

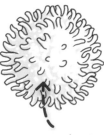

pom pom body

5 For the sheep, glue two pom poms to the hills. Cut out black felt heads and glue them into position. Finally, staple your hill landscape, facedown, to the back of your frame.

Why not try making a picture of the scene outside your window?

HESSIAN POT WRAP

Work on your embroidery skills and brighten up a dull flower pot with this pretty wrap.

1 Gather the hessian fabric around the flower pot and tie it up at the top with a ribbon tied into a bow.

2 Using the tailors' chalk, draw a tree design on one side of the hessian fabric. At the ends of the tree branches, draw circular shapes.

96

3 Begin your embroidery by using back stitch to outline the tree trunk. Embroider the circles using colourful thread and a variety of stitches, such as chain stitch and satin stitch.

4 Sew on assorted beads and buttons to add a decorative finish.

Wrapped around a beautiful plant, this would make a wonderful Mother's Day gift.

BOUNCY BIRD

Hang this feathered friend next to your window in your room.

1 Wrap two elastic bands around a polystyrene ball so they cross over each other. Using wool threaded onto an embroidery needle, thread the wool over and around the elastic bands. (See page 80 for a similar method.)

2 Keep weaving until the ball is covered, changing wool colours to make a stripy effect. Tie a knot in your last thread and cut off the excess. You could leave some wool threads loose to attach beads for decoration.

3 Make a pair of wings by cutting out four identical wing shapes from felt. Sew the pairs together with running stitch. Leave a space to insert a small amount of toy stuffing, then sew closed.

4 To make a tail, glue feathers onto the back of your bird. Glue the stiff quills under a section of woven wool. Glue or sew the wings onto the sides of the body.

5 Glue on a folded diamond felt beak and add goggly eyes. Stitch a length of elastic thread to the ridge at the top so you can hang your bird.

Make your bird in colours that match your bedroom!

99

POOCH PUPPET

This soft puppet is just as cute and cuddly as a real dog – but not as much work!

1 Fill a sock with toy stuffing and insert a pipe cleaner through the middle, so it is contained inside. Tie 3 elastic bands at regular spaces to create round body sections.

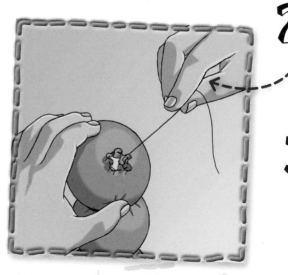

2 Sew a line of loose running stitch around the opening and pull the end of the thread until the opening gathers together.

3 Sew a line of running stitch all the way down the back of the sock body.

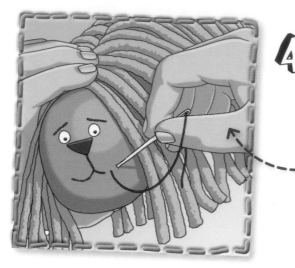

4 To make the pooch's fur, thread each length of wool through the running stitches along the back, using a large embroidery needle. Embroider a nose, mouth and eyebrows onto the face. Stick on goggly eyes.

5 Cut out two felt ears and sew these onto the head. Sew the bell onto a length of ribbon and tie around the pooch's neck. Finally, make a small hole in the underside of the head, and push one dowel rod into the hole. Repeat at the other end of the body.

Make a family of pooches using different coloured socks and wool.

DRAWING MATERIALS

wax crayons

drawing pencil

Drawing pencils

An HB pencil is recommended to begin with and then try B and 2B for softer shading. Don't try to shade with an H pencil as it is too hard. "H" pencils get harder as the numbers go up, and "B" pencils get softer as the numbers go up.

Coloured pencils

Coloured pencils come in a huge variety of colours. Generally they are similar in hardness, but soft ones that can be smudged and blended are available too.

Watercolour pencils

Watercolour pencils look very similar to normal coloured pencils, but they are soluble in water, which will give your drawings a watercolour effect. You can either dip them in water before drawing or colour as normal and then brush water over the top.

Wax crayons

Wax crayons are sticks of coloured wax. They come in many colours and are great to use for rubbings as they are typically very blunt, which is good for shading large areas of colour. They are also waterproof, so you can paint over the top and the wax colour will show clearly through and will not run.

Inks

Drawing inks can be bought in small bottles. They can be diluted with water and applied with a brush or pen. Interesting effects can be created by

inks

dropping small blobs of ink onto wet paper and letting them flow. An ink pad is good for fingerprinting and can be made easily with a small piece of sponge lightly soaked with ink.

Pens and markers

There are many different kinds of pens and markers available in different thicknesses and colours. Try experimenting with as many as possible to create lines, shading, textures and patterns.

For detailed work try fineliners in sizes 0.1mm, 0.3mm, 0.5mm and 0.7mm. For thicker marks, try markers that have broader nibs.

Permanent markers are generally resistant to rubbing and water, but won't wash off most surfaces so you have to be very careful with them.

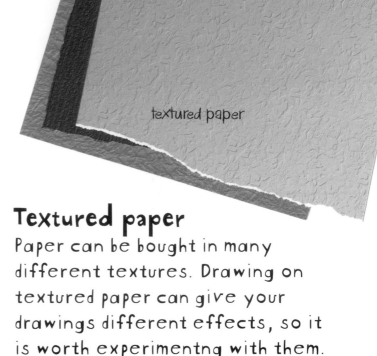
textured paper

Textured paper

Paper can be bought in many different textures. Drawing on textured paper can give your drawings different effects, so it is worth experimentng with them.

glitter glue

Glitter glue

Glitter glue can be bought in a bottle with a fine nozzle and is suitable for drawing fine lines.

permanent marker

fineliner

felt-tip pens

coloured pencils

PAINTING MATERIALS

Acrylic paint

Acrylic paint comes in tubes. It is quite thick and a little can go a long way, so only use a small amount. You can thin it with water, but the colours are more vibrant if you use it without. When acrylic paint dries, you cannot lift it off with water. It can only be painted over. It has a glue-like surface, once dry, that is waterproof.

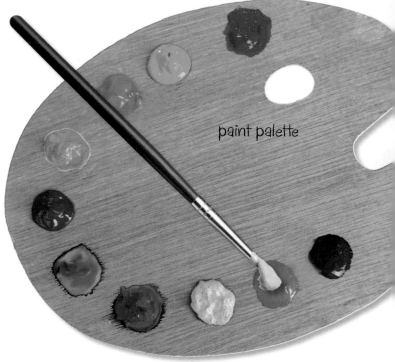

paint palette

Cartridge paper

Cartridge paper is an excellent choice for pencil and pen drawings. It comes in different thicknesses. The thicker versions will withstand being painted. Watercolour paper is specially designed for watercolour paints. It has a wonderful texture that is perfect for the delicacy of watercolour painting.

Paint palette

A paint palette is a special surface used for mixing different colours of paint. Paint palettes can be place mats, a piece of acrylic glass, a paper plate or cardboard covered in wax paper.

cartridge papers

Watercolour paints

Watercolour paints can be bought as blocks with a palette or in small tubes. If you buy tubes, only squeeze a small amount onto a palette and mix with water. If using blocks, wet a paintbrush and stroke over the block and paint onto a palette. The more water you use, the lighter the colour. If you want a very intense colour, use only a little water – just enough to lift the colour from the block.

Paintbrushes

Paintbrushes come in many different shapes and sizes – round or flat, thick or thin. Use the right type of paintbrush for the kind of painting you are doing.

paintbrushes

acrylic paint

Small paintbrushes are ideal for adding detail and large, flat brushes are good for big, sweeping strokes. Clean brushes after you use them and they will last for a long time.

Materials to add texture

Texture can be added to paint using many different methods. Try mixing things like sand and glitter into your paint. You can add texture using PVA glue, letting it dry and painting over the top. You can also paint with other tools besides paintbrushes, like sponges, cotton buds and even your fingers!

watercolour paints

Sponge

105

PRINTING MATERIALS

sponge brush

Poster paint

Poster paints are good for projects that are printed on paper. But they do not mix well to make new colours.

Fabric paint

Fabric paints are best for printing onto fabric, as they will not wash off or bleed into the material. They will need fixing with a hot iron before washing, but always make sure an adult does this for you. Make sure whatever you are painting onto has been washed first. Acrylic paint can also be used for printing on fabric, such as shoes or bags. It does not need to be heat set but will dry stiffer than fabric paint.

poster paint

Sponge brush

A sponge brush is best when painting onto objects that are to be used to print with, because it will absorb excess paint. Use a sponge brush when the printing object is too large to fit onto a stamp pad.

Adhesive foam sheets

These are thick sheets of a lightweight but tough, bendy material, that are adhesive on one side. You can cut them into shapes and they bend without tearing.

fabric paint

adhesive foam sheet

coloured paper

Coloured paper

Paper can be bought in many colours. Using coloured paper can give your creations different effects, so it is worth experimenting with them. Almost any kind of paper can be used with these projects, as long as it can withstand being painted.

Work preparation

It's important to cover the work surface with plastic or paper to prevent any permanent accidents and to make cleaning up easier. Inexpensive plastic tablecloths work well. Also, wearing an old shirt or an apron is a good idea to protect clothing. Be sure to have some baby wipes or paper towels handy to clean up any spills or messy hands.

Printing objects

Almost anything can be used to print with, as long as you ask permission first and it can withstand being painted. Plastic toys and fruit and vegetables make great printing objects, as does anything with an interesting pattern or texture.

Floral foam (oasis)

Floral foam is available from florists and garden centres. It is great to make a stamp from as it is very stiff and easy to carve designs into.

floral foam

OTHER MATERIALS

embroidery thread

wool

Embroidery thread

This is a type of yarn used especially for embroidery. It comes in loads of different colours.

Needles and pins

pins

Needles are pointed metal tools to sew with. They have a hole at the top called an 'eye' to thread yarn through. Pins are very similar to needles but don't have an eye at the top. They are used to hold fabric in place before sewing. Always ask an adult to help you with needles and pins. They can be very sharp.

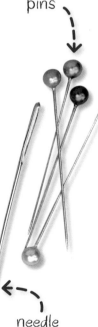

needle

Wool

Wool is like very thick yarn that comes in many different colours and thicknesses. It is usually used for knitting, but can be used for weaving and even embroidery.

Toy stuffing

This is soft, white material, similar to cotton wool. It is great for padding out your creations, to help them look more 3D. It also makes toys soft and cuddly!

toy stuffing

PVA glue

PVA (Polyvinyl acetate) is a widely-used, safe type of glue which is great for sticking paper, card, wood and almost anything. It is sometimes called white glue or school glue. PVA usually comes in a squeezy bottle with a nozzle, which makes it very clean and easy to use.

PVA glue

Dowel rods

Dowel rods are solid, lightweight sticks used for adding support to your creations. They are usually made of wood or plastic. They are easy to cut to size, but always ask an adult to do this for you.

dowel rods

Tailors' chalk

Tailors' chalk is a very hard type of chalk that is used to make marks on fabric. It is useful to draw out shapes that you need to cut out. The marks can be washed off.

tailors' chalk

Foam sheets

These are thick sheets of a lightweight but tough,

felt

bendy material. You can cut them into shapes, glue them and bend them without them tearing.

foam sheet

Fabric glue

Fabric glue is the best glue to stick fabrics together, as it can be washed without coming unstuck.

Fabric

Fabric is any type of cloth. You can use old clothes to make your creations from, but always ask an adult before cutting anything up!

fabrics

Felt

This is a type of cloth that is usually soft and comes in loads of different colours. It is strong and will not fray when cut.

DRAWING TECHNIQUES

Tips on cross hatching

1. Keep your pencil well sharpened and try not to grip it too tightly. Begin with simple strokes all in the same direction, lifting the pencil up between each stroke.

2. Make long, light strokes with the side of the pencil point. Don't press too hard. If the strokes are too short they begin to look like furry caterpillars.

3. Make another layer of shading over the first in a different direction.

4. Repeat with a third layer in a different direction. Each different direction adds more tone to the shading, and makes it progressively darker and darker.

5. Velvety strokes can be used to finish off areas of shading. Glide the pencil back and forth very lightly over the darkest areas.

6. To make furry strokes, try holding the pencil a long way from its point. Hold it loosely and waggle it across the paper.

Shading
Lines or other marks used to show gradual changes of colour or darkness.

Texture
The appearance and feel of a surface.

Colour blending
You can use the cross hatching method to overlap and blend coloured pencils together.

Colours which are close on the colour circle blend well together. For example, reds, oranges and yellows, blues, greens and yellows, or pinks, purples and blues.

Collage
A collage may include newspaper clippings, pieces of fabric, bits of coloured or hand-made papers, portions of other artwork or words, photographs and other objects. These can be glued onto paper or canvas in an arrangement of your choice.

Frottage
In frottage the artist takes a pencil or other drawing tool and makes a "rubbing" over a textured surface. The drawing can be left as it is or worked into.

Frottage can be made by laying sheets of paper over the surface and then rubbing over them with a soft pencil. It is best to keep the pencil lines in the same direction and to use the side of the point.

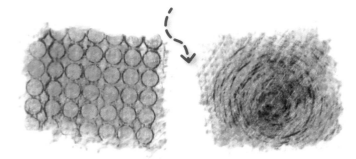

Perspective
Perspective rules help artists to draw in such a way as to make objects appear to be 3D. Remember that objects appear to be smaller when they are in the distance.

Experimenting
Trying things out to see what will happen.

PAINTING TECHNIQUES

Using watercolour

To apply colour, use light colours first, then build up to darker colours. Let the paint dry before adding more, unless you want the colours to bleed and mix together.

If you paint a colour onto paper, but decide you want it lighter, you can add water with a paintbrush to lift the paint off.

It is a good idea to use thick paper with watercolours, as you tend to use more water. Paper can only take so much water before it begins to break up.

Using acrylic

To mix colours, always start with the lightest colour on the palette. Add a little of the darker colour at a time, until you are happy with the colour you have mixed.

When painting, think about the direction of your strokes. Sometimes you can see the marks of brush hairs moving in a direction. Also think about the length of your strokes. Do you want long, sweeping strokes or quick, short flicks?

Using pencils

When drawing, use a light pressure on your pencil. If your pencil marks are too dark they may show through or mix with the paint. If pencil marks are too dark, simply use an eraser to lighten them before painting.

Adding texture

To add a grainy texture, mix a small amount of sand or glitter with your paint before use.

To add a pattern, texture or design with PVA glue, apply the PVA in the pattern or texture you want, allow it to dry completely and then paint over the top. PVA glue often comes in a squeezy bottle with a nozzle to make this easier.

To apply paint with a sponge, a cotton bud or fabric, dip the item into a small amount of paint and then dab it onto paper.

Wax painting

When you paint on top of wax with a thin water-based paint, such as watercolour, an interesting effect happens. Because the paint cannot stick to the wax, you will be able to see the wax drawing through the paint. You can use a candle to draw with before applying the paint, but remember you won't be able to see what you are drawing! You can also use coloured wax crayons to achieve this effect.

Transferring a tracing

To transfer a tracing on tracing paper onto paper, turn the tracing paper onto its back and carefully draw over the lines in pencil. Next, flip the tracing paper back onto the right side and lay a sheet of paper underneath it. Carefully draw over the tracing with a heavy pressure on your pencil.
The tracing should now have transferred onto the paper.

Sgraffito

With this technique you can scratch through paint to reveal a layer of colour underneath. Apply blocks of bold colour to thick paper with oil pastels, then apply a thick layer of ready-made paint over the top. Once dry, carefully scratch the paint away with a sharp object.

113

PRINTING TECHNIQUES

Applying paint

Paint is applied to the stamps and printing tools in different ways, depending on the tool or technique being used.

A sponge brush is used to apply paint to roller printing tools or to large printing plates. When the stamp is too big for a stamp pad, such as vegetable stamps or toys, a sponge brush is also used. Dip the sponge brush into paint and apply it to the item.

For small or delicate items, like floral foam stamps or modelling clay stamps, press them onto a stamp pad to apply the paint. If paint is applied with a sponge brush, it will clog up the carved design lines.

With foam or sponge stamps, a small amount of paint is put onto a paint palette. The foam or sponge stamp is dipped into the paint until the bottom surface is covered. A fat paintbrush is used to apply paint for stencilling.

Pour a small amount of paint into a plastic cup, dip the brush into the paint, then hold the stencil flat with one hand and tap the brush around the edges and open areas of the stencil. Do this until all of the open spaces of the stencil have been filled in.

Making a stamp pad

Some stamps, such as those made from modelling clay or floral foam, work best with a foam stamp pad that you can make yourself. Put a small sponge on top of a plastic lid. (If it's the type of sponge that is hard when dry, wet it first to soften it, then squeeze out all of the water.) Squeeze a small amount of paint onto the sponge, then use your fingers to spread it around. Use it just like a normal stamp pad, but add more paint as needed. Wash out the sponge when you are done.

Stencilling

Stencilling prints the negative spaces of a design. You can either make your own stencils out of paper, or use things like masking tape and stickers. Objects like bubble wands or plastic toys can also be used as stencils. Stencils are great to use when you want to repeat a design for a project.

Gluing

Glue can be used to create a rubbing plate or it can be used to attach thick wool to cardboard to create a printing plate. For a rubbing plate, draw a picture onto a piece of cardboard, then trace over the picture with glue. Once dry, place paper on top of the rubbing plate and scribble over it with crayons to make the design appear. You can use as many colours as you want, overlapping them, or only use one colour.

Toothbrush spatter paint

Spatter painting with a toothbrush looks like splattered spray paint but uses a toothbrush and paint. Squirt a small amount of paint onto an old toothbrush then, with the bristles facing down, run your finger across the bristles towards you to spatter paint on the project. Use several colours for different coloured spatters.

Monoprinting

Use this technique when you only want to make one print. It involves drawing directly into the paint on a paint palette. Spread a thin layer of paint onto a paint palette with a sponge brush, then draw a design into the paint with your finger, a paintbrush or the eraser end of a pencil. Remember that everything will print backwards, so if you want any writing, it needs to be backwards too. Place the printed side of the paint palette onto the project, pressing down on it to be sure the whole design prints, then carefully remove it.

OTHER TECHNIQUES

MAKE A POM POM

YOU WILL NEED:
- Scissors
- Cardboard
- Wool

1 Cut two identical doughnut rings from cardboard and place them together.

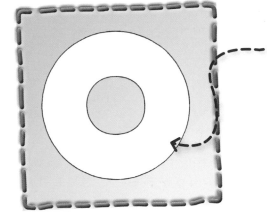

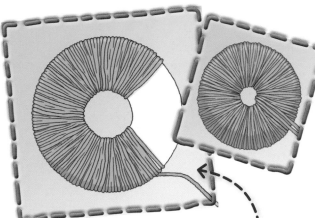

2 Wrap the wool around the rings, going through the hole and around the outer edge. Keep wrapping until the hole in the middle is very tight.

3 Cut through the wool around the edge of the ring, a layer at a time, until you meet the cardboard rings underneath.

4 Pass a length of wool inbetween the two cardboard rings. Tie it tightly around all the wool at the centre. Now remove the cardbaord rings and reveal your pom pom!

116

STITCHING AND WEAVING

Running stitch

Sew up and down through the fabric, making sure the stitches on both the topside and underside are kept the same size.

Blanket stitch

Push the needle through from back to front. At the front, level with your first stitch, push the needle through the fabric but come up again by going through the loop you have created with the thread.

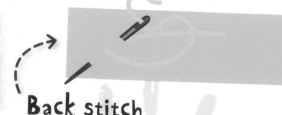

Back stitch

Make a running stitch, then come up through the fabric a stitch ahead and stitch backwards to meet your first running stitch. Repeat in a neat line.

Weaving

Lengths of material are passed through a set of taut, spaced-out threads, in an alternate 'over, under, over, under' pattern. This is repeated with many lengths so that they make an interlacing lattice. You can also weave 'over and around' dowel rods in a cross shape (see woven mobile on page 80).

Chain stitch

Come up through the fabric and make a little loop, held in place with your thumb. Go back down through the fabric at the top and inside the loop. Come back up and forward a stitch length. Before pulling the needle all the way out, wrap the free thread under the needle and pull out to create your second loop.

Satin stitch

Mark out the shape you want and sew straight stitches closely together across the shape, taking care to keep the edges even.

INDEX

INDEX